Start Playing
CHESS

Rosalyn B. Katz

Sterling Publishing Co., Inc.
New York

Dedicated to my son Steven M. Katz

Library of Congress Cataloging-in-Publication Data

Katz, Rosalyn B., 1943–
   [Chess for Children]
   Start playing chess / Rosalyn B. Katz.
       p.   cm.
   Originally published: Chess for children. London : Collins & Brown, 1993.
   Includes index.
   ISBN 0-8069-9349-9
   1. Chess for children—Juvenile literature.   I. Title.
GV1446.K38   1996
794.1'2—dc20
                                           96-24656
                                                  CIP
                                                   AC

2 4 6 8 10 9 7 5 3 1

Published 1996 by Sterling Publishing Company, Inc.
387 Park Avenue South, New York, N.Y. 10016
Originally published in Great Britain & © 1993 under the title
Chess for Children by Collins & Brown Limited and Cadogan Books Limited
Text © 1993 by Rosalyn B. Katz
Distributed in Canada by Sterling Publishing
% Canadian Manda Group, One Atlantic Avenue, Suite 105
Toronto, Ontario, Canada M6K 3E7
Manufactured in the United States of America
All rights reserved

Sterling ISBN 0-8069-9349-9

Contents

1 The Game

To play chess you must think and plan.
BRAIN POWER is the key to winning.

There are two players, known as White (who moves the white pieces) and Black (who moves the black pieces). Each player wants to capture the other's King.

Important things to know

- Each piece occupies one square. The pieces can move to different squares, but can only take an enemy square by capturing the piece that's on it.

- Check — attack the enemy King.

- Checkmate (or mate) — attack the enemy King so that it cannot escape.

- Capture — bump an enemy piece off the board by moving your piece onto its square.

- Move — each player gets a turn to move one piece at a time. (Except when castling — but we'll talk about that later.) The player with the white pieces gets to move first.

To play you need a board and pieces.

The object of the game is to checkmate the enemy King. "Mate" it — so it can't escape.

Check

You are in check when your King is attacked by an enemy piece. You must get out of check right away.

Ways to get out of check

♚	Block	put another piece in the way
♚	Capture	take away the enemy piece
♚	Move	put the King on a safe square

Checkmate

When a King is in check and has no way to get out of check, the game is over. Checkmate or "mate."

Stalemate/Draw

When there are no remaining legal moves on the board and neither King is in check, it is stalemate. Nobody wins—it's a draw.

It's also a draw if...

the same position is repeated three times during the game with the same player to move each time;

or

there are not enough pieces to mate;

or

both players agree to a draw.

Resignation

When a player has a horrible position, with no way to win or draw, that player may resign. That also means the game is over.

Sometimes players agree to a draw — and go play tennis.

... or start another game.

A chess game starts when White makes the first move... and ends when:

White wins (Score: 1 — 0)
Black wins (Score: 0 — 1)
Draw (Score: ½ — ½).

2   The Board

The board is the world of the chess pieces.

The chess board has light and dark squares.

A light square is always in the bottom right corner.

Light on right.

The numbers
go up the side.

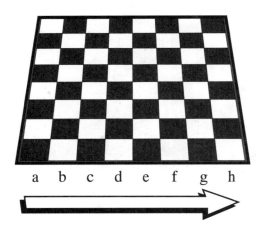

The letters go
across the
bottom.

To find d6,
go right to d,
and up to 6.

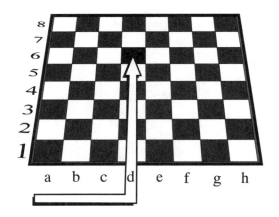

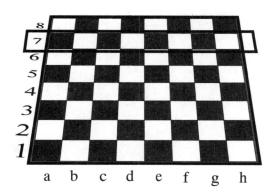

Each row on the chess board is called a rank. The row numbered 7 is called the 7th rank.

Each column of a chess board is called a file. The "a" file is the left-most file on the board.

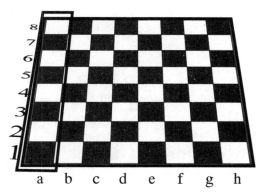

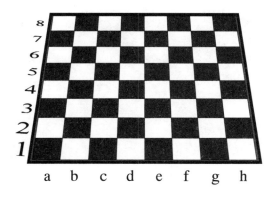

Put a ✔ on square e5.

Did you find e5?

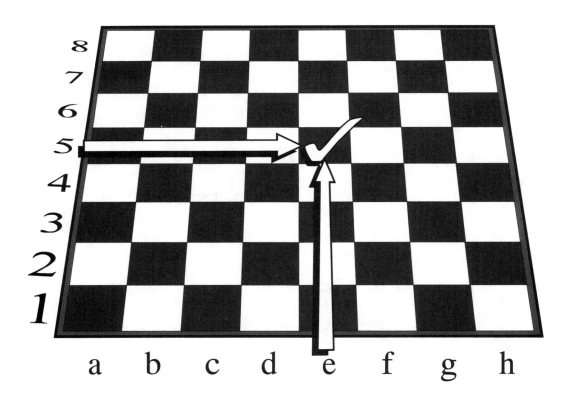

If you found e5, go to the next chapter to learn about the pieces.
If you did not find e5, go back to page 6 and read it again.

3   The Pieces

The pieces always start on the same squares.

NAME	SYMBOL	LETTER
Knight	♞	N
Rook	♜	R
Bishop	♝	B
Queen	♛	Q
King	♚	K
Pawn	♟	a, b, c, d, e, f, g, h

The pawn is known
by the letter
of its file.

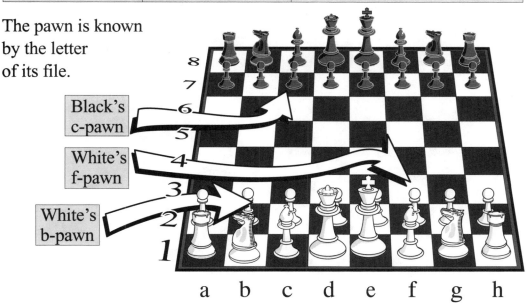

Black's c-pawn

White's f-pawn

White's b-pawn

Each piece has a different job and makes different moves.

You are the boss of all your pieces like a conductor telling musicians how to play.

... or a coach managing a team.

When your pieces work together to protect your King and to beat the enemy, you win.

Some pieces have more power than others.		
Piece		**Value in Pawns**
Q	♕	9 ♙♙♙♙♙♙♙♙♙
R	♖	5 ♙♙♙♙♙
B	♗	3 ♙♙♙
N	♘	3 ♙♙♙

The Knight

N

The Knights start on these squares.

b1 and g1 for White

b8 and g8 for Black

The Knight is the only piece that can jump over other pieces. It moves two squares in one direction, and one square in another direction.

This Knight can go to a3 or c3 or d2.

The Knight always winds up on a different-color square from where it started.

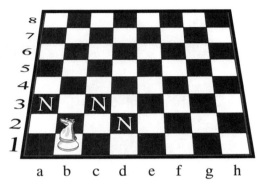

The arrows show all the squares that the Knight on d4 can move to.

A Knight in the middle of the board has eight possible moves.

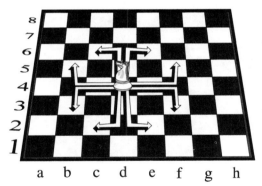

This Knight can move from c4 to d2. Two squares down and one square right.

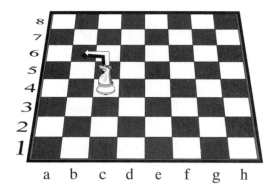

The Knight can also move from c4 to b6. Two squares up and one square left.

The Knight can also move from c4 to b2. Two squares down and one square left.

The Knight attacks any piece that is on a square that it can move to. To capture an opponent's piece, the Knight replaces the opponent's piece. The captured piece is taken off the board.

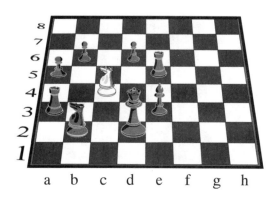

The Knight on c4 can capture any of these pieces.

Put an "N" on each square where the Knight on e6 can move.

A)

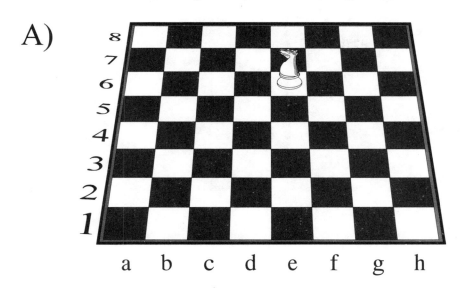

Put X's on all pieces that can be captured by the black Knight on e7.

B)

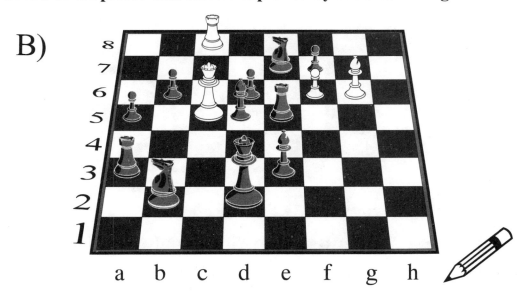

A)

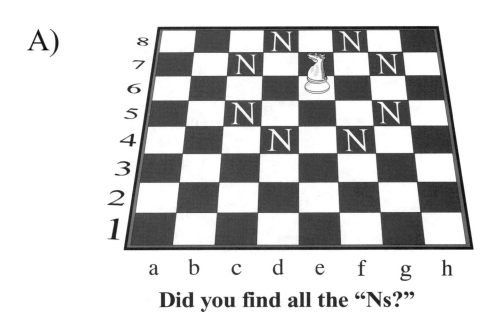

Did you find all the "Ns?"

B)

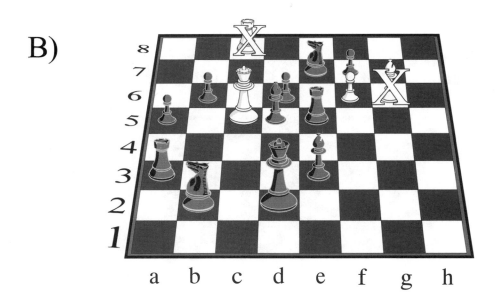

Did you remember that the Knight can jump over pieces and it captures only enemy pieces?

The Rook

R

The Rooks start on these squares.

a1 and h1 for White

a8 and h8 for Black

The Rook moves straight up, down, or sideways any number of squares: a1 to h1 or a1 to a8. Like this.

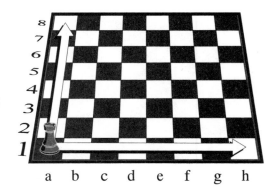

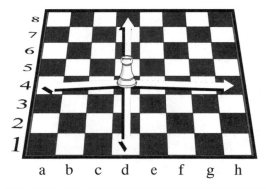

Or this.

The Rook attacks any piece directly in its path. The Rook captures the same way as it moves. The Rook cannot jump over another piece. It stops before it hits the other piece, or it captures the enemy piece. When it is moved to a square that contains an opponent's piece, it replaces that piece and the piece is removed from the board.

Here it can capture the Queen
or the Pawn
or the Knight
or the Bishop.

A) Put an "R" on all the squares the c5 Rook can go.

B) Put an "X" on all pieces that the Rook on e4 can capture.

-19-

A)

Did you find all the "R" squares?

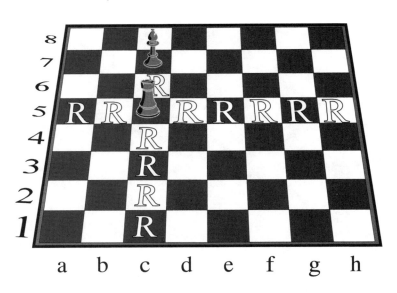

B)

Did you mark the Bishop on e6?

The Bishop

B

The Bishops start on these squares.

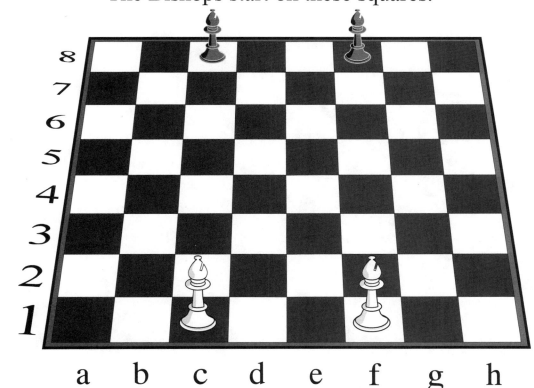

c1 and f1 for White

c8 and f8 for Black

The Bishop moves diagonally. It cannot move straight up and down or sideways; it moves diagonally, always on the same-color square. Like this.

c1 to a3 or c1 to h6 or any squares along the way.

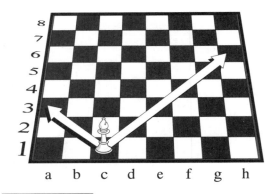

Remember, it cannot jump over another piece. Only the Knight can do that.

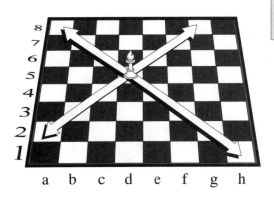

Or this.

It stays on the same color for the whole game. The "light" Bishop must always land on a light square. The "dark" Bishop must always land on a dark square.

The Bishop attacks any piece in its path. The Bishop captures the same way it moves. When it captures the enemy piece, it takes over its square.

A)

Put a "B" on every square the e5 Bishop can go to.

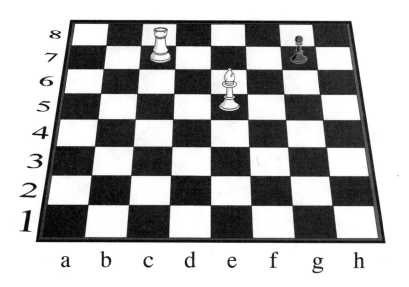

B)

Which pieces can the White Bishop capture?

A)

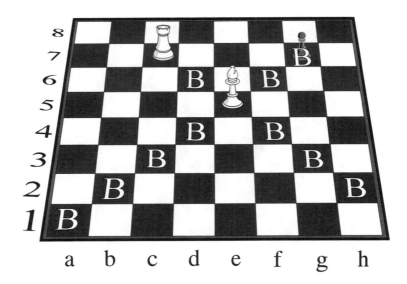

Did you find all the "B" squares?
Did you remember that the Bishop cannot jump over pieces but can capture an enemy piece?

B)

The Queen

Q

The Queens start on d1 for White and d8 for Black.

The White Queen starts on a light square.

The Black Queen starts on a dark square.

The Queen is the strongest
piece on the board.

It can move like a Bishop
or a Rook.

Like this:

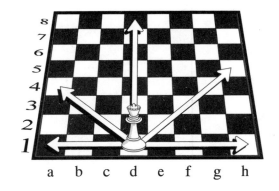

Or this:

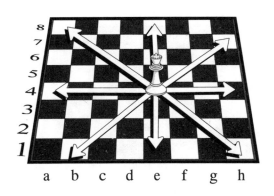

The Queen attacks any piece
directly in its path.

The Queen captures the same
way that it moves.

The Queen cannot jump
over other pieces.

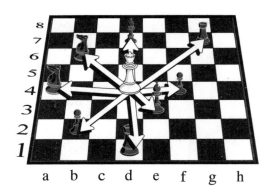

A)

Put a "Q" on all the squares the d4 Queen can go.

B)

Which pieces can the White Queen capture?

A)

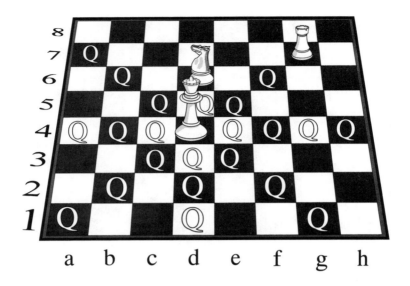

Did you find all the "Q" squares?

B)

The Pawn

P

The pawns start across the second rank for White
and across the seventh rank for Black.

Pawns move only forward, never backward.
The pawn moves straight ahead, one square at a time
—except on its first move or when it captures a piece.

Pawns do strange things.

Pawns:

♟ can move one or two squares on their first move

♟ turn into other pieces when getting all the way across the board

♟ move forward but capture diagonally

♟ change their names after capturing

♟ pretend the enemy pawn moved one square instead of two in the special "en passant" move

When the pawn first moves, it goes one or two squares.

The e-pawn goes to e3 or e4.

The pawn is named for the file that it's on (a, b, c, d, e, f, g, or h).

After its first move, a pawn can move only one square at a time.

Put an "e" on all the squares this pawn can move.

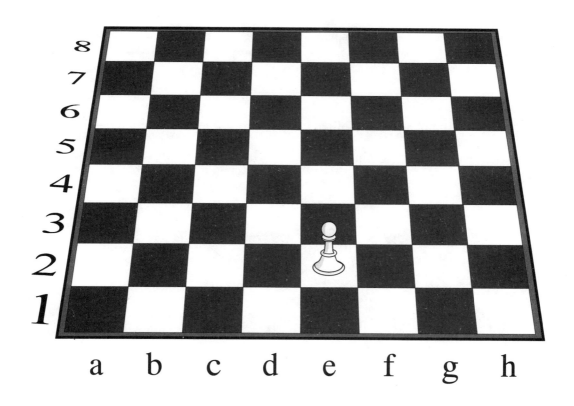

Did you find e3 and e4?

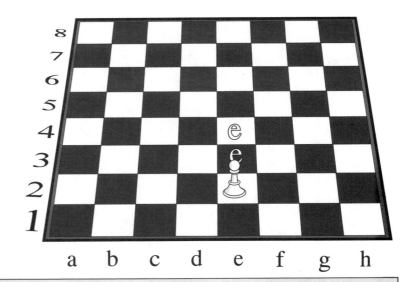

A pawn attacks a piece when that piece is one square diagonally ahead of it. When a pawn captures an enemy piece, it moves diagonally one square—replacing the piece it captures.

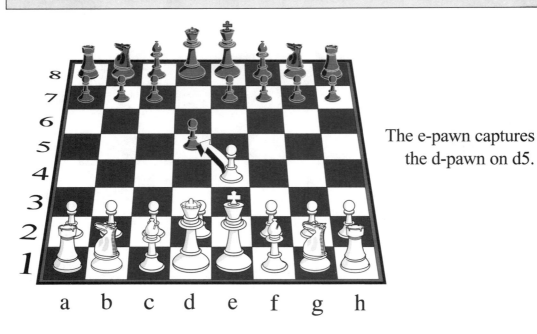

The e-pawn captures the d-pawn on d5.

A pawn cannot capture the piece on the square directly in front of it.

Put an "X" on all the pieces that can be captured by the e-pawn.

**Good,
if you marked the Knight on f3.**

When a pawn is successful
in moving all the way to
the other end of a file
it turns into a Queen
(or any other piece you
pick except a King).

En Passant

Capturing "en passant" (in passing) happens only with pawns.

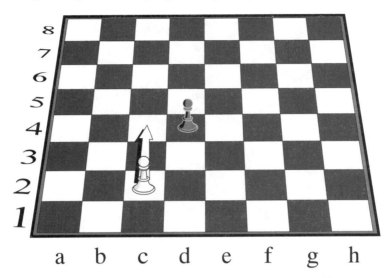

If a pawn on its start square moves two squares landing next to an enemy pawn, it can be captured as if it moved only one square. The capture must happen right away.

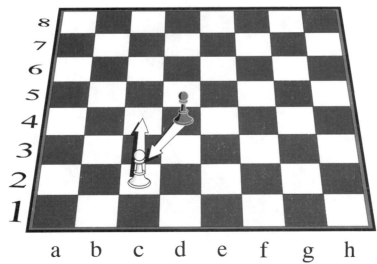

The Black d-pawn captures the White c-pawn on c3.

The King

K

The Kings start on e1 for White and e8 for Black.

They face each other across the board.

You have to take really good care of your King. It is *the most important* piece in chess.

The King moves only one square at a time, but can move in any direction.

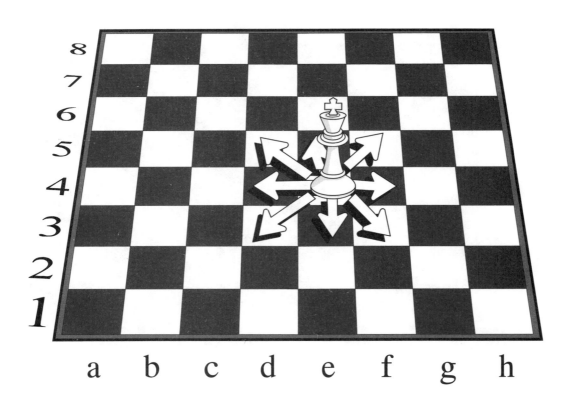

It can not move to a square where it will be in check.

Put a "K" on all the squares this c3 King can go.

Did you find all the "K" squares?
The King could not move to the "d"
file because it would be in check.

The King can capture a piece on any square that is next to it, as long as the King will not be in check.

Put an "X" on the pieces the White King can capture.

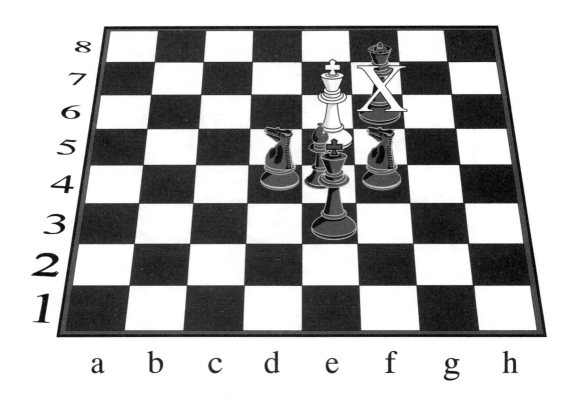

Only the Black Queen!

The other Black pieces are protected.

The White King can't capture them because

it would be in check.

Castling

Castling is the only time two pieces move at once.

The King and Rook.

It is the only time a King moves more than one square and the only time a Rook jumps over a King.

You can NOT castle if:

 the King is in check

 the King or Rook has been moved earlier in the game

 other pieces are in the way

 the King must pass through check on any of the squares

To castle Kingside.

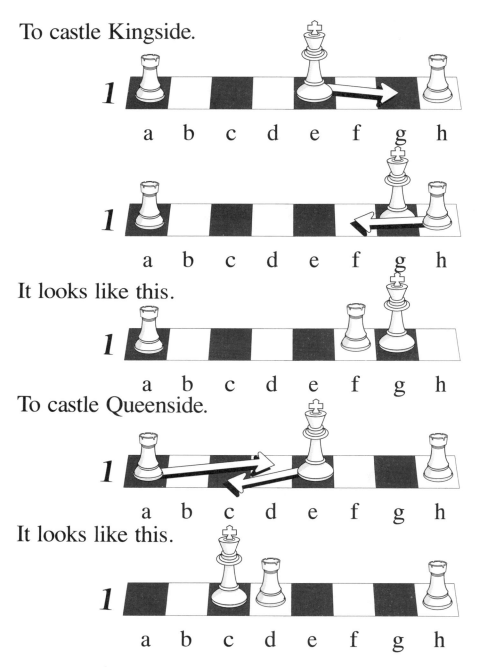

It looks like this.

To castle Queenside.

It looks like this.

Remember: Move the King two squares toward the
Rook and put the Rook on the other side of the King.

A) Castle Kingside (shown by O — O) by putting a K and R to show the castled position below.

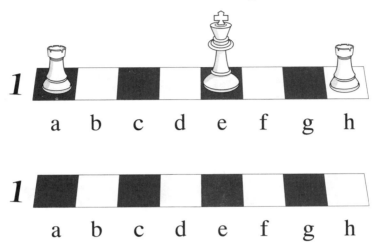

B) Now castle Queenside (O — O — O).

A) O—O

B) O—O—O

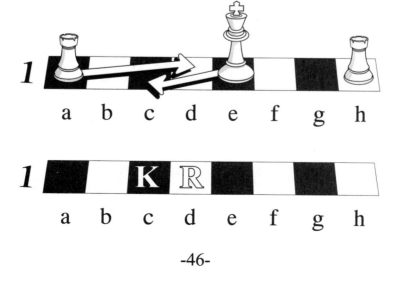

4 Mates and Attacks

Here are some simple positions for you to look at. Since you need to "mate" to win, this chapter will help you to set up winning positions. Write on the pages where you see pencils to show where the pieces go. Draw an arrow to show how you're moving a piece. You turn the page to find the best answer.

A good idea is to use a board and pieces to work out the problems.

In the diagram above, White moves. Find how White mates in one move.

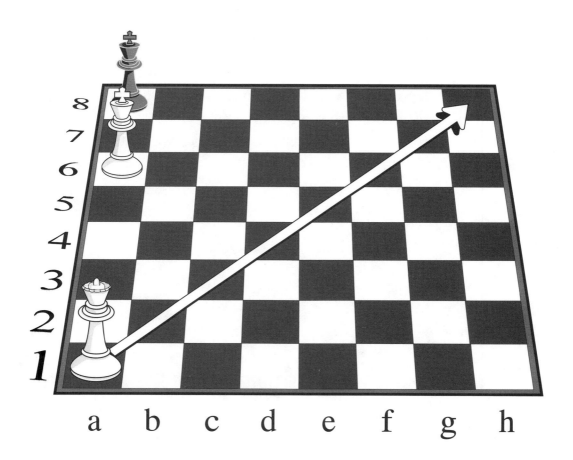

A)

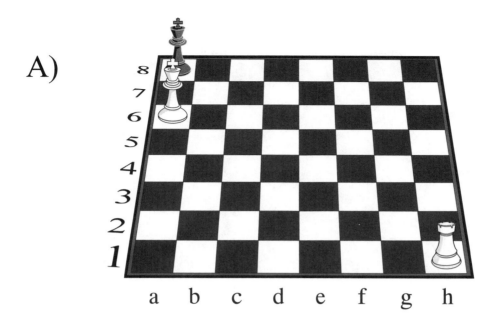

White moves. Find how White mates in one.

B)

White moves. Find how White mates in one move.

A)

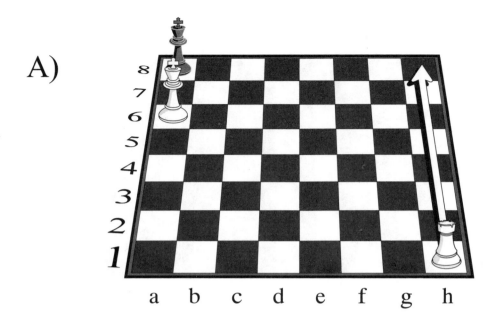

B)

-50-

A)

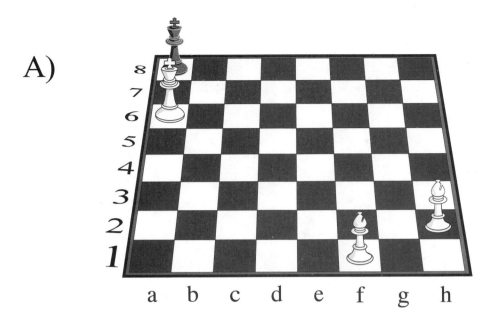

Black to move — what happens now?

B)

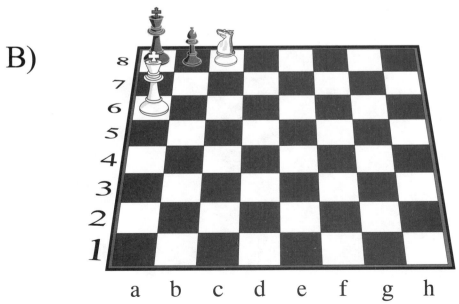

White moves. Find the mate.

A)

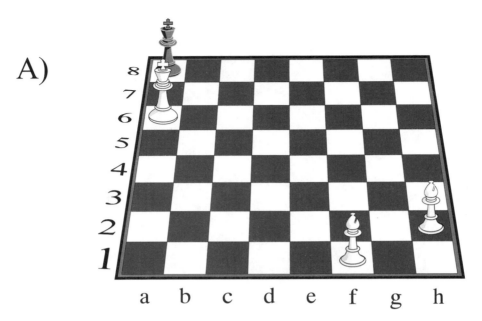

If it is Black to move, it's a draw. Black has no legal move and is stalemated.

B)

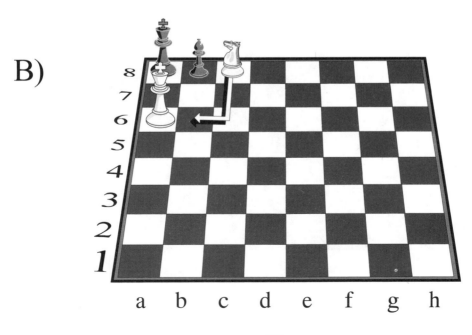

A)

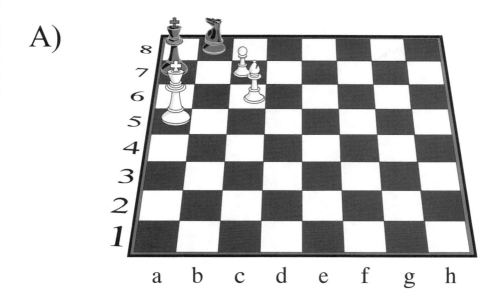

White moves. Find how White mates in one move.

B)

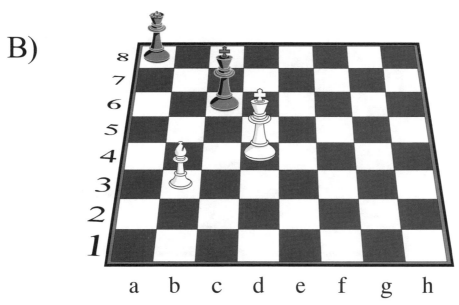

If White moves, what is best?

A)

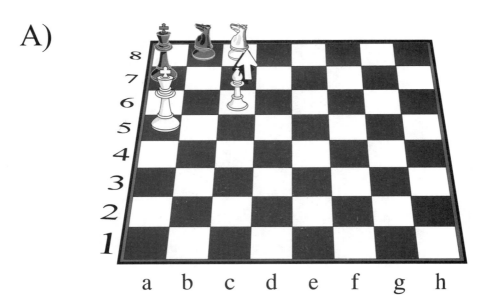

The c-pawn promotes to a Knight, instead of the usual Queen.
A Knight would "mate" the Black King.

B)

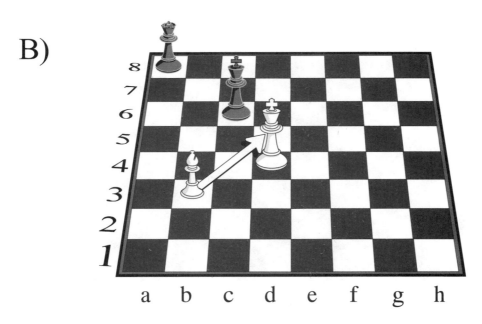

Now Black's King is in check. When the King moves the Bishop can
capture the Queen.

A)

What is the best move for Black?

B)

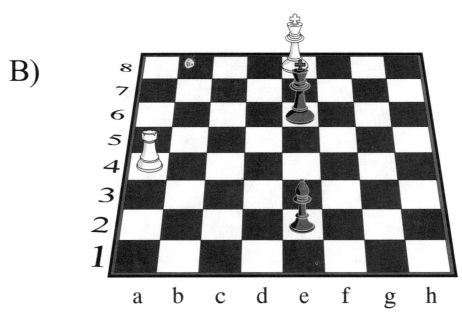

Black moves. What is the best move?

A)

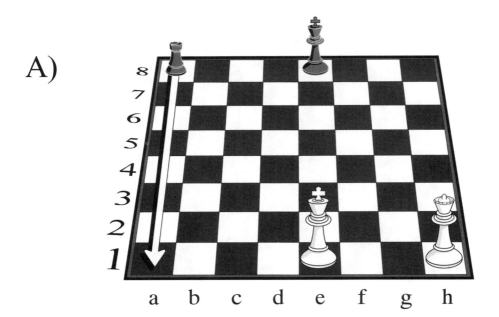

Black will capture the Queen.

B)

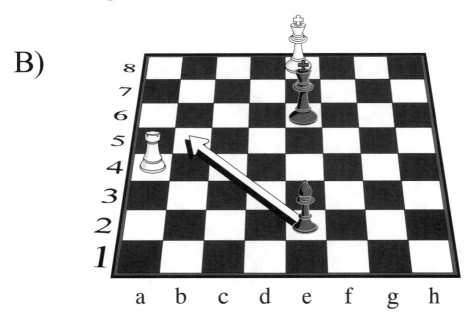

Now White's King is in check.
When the King moves the Bishop can capture the Rook.

White moves.
What's the best move?

Now Black's King is in check.
When the King moves
the Rook can capture the Bishop.

5 Writing the Games

This section teaches you how to keep a record of the moves. You can get a score book to write the moves, or just write them on a piece of paper. You write your games so that you can:

- ♛ go over them
- ♛ learn from your mistakes
- ♛ show them off!!!

To write or read games, you need to know the letters and symbols used

The Pieces

WRITE	MEANING
K	King
Q	Queen
R	Rook
B	Bishop
N	Knight
a, b, c, d, e, f, g, h	Pawn

The Moves

SYMBOL	MEANING
X	captures
+	check
++	checkmate
!	good move
!!	great move
?	bad move
??	rotten move
?!	may be bad
!?	interesting
0–0	castles Kingside
0–0–0	castles Queenside

Reading the moves.

...c5

This means that Black (...) moved the c-pawn to c5.

exf6

This means that the e-pawn (White) captured on f6.

0-0-0

This means White
castled Queenside.

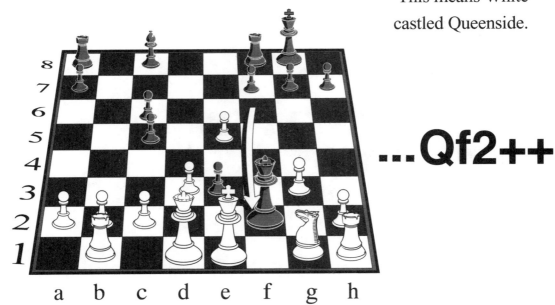

...Qf2++

This means Queen
to f2 checkmate.

Write the moves shown by the arrows.

A)

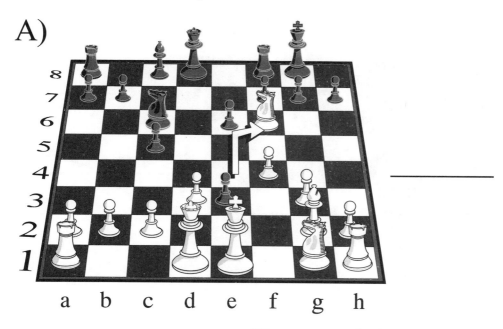

_____

There was a Black Bishop on f6 above.

B)

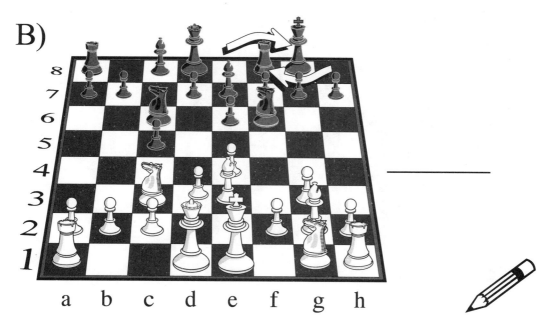

_____

Is this how you wrote the moves?

A)

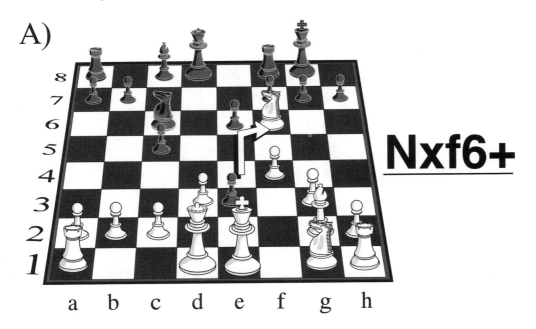

Nxf6+

B)

...0-0

Write the moves shown by the arrows.

A)

B)

There was a White Knight on f6.

Is this how you wrote the moves?

A)

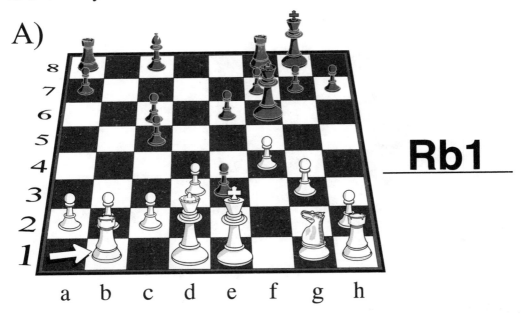

Rb1

B)

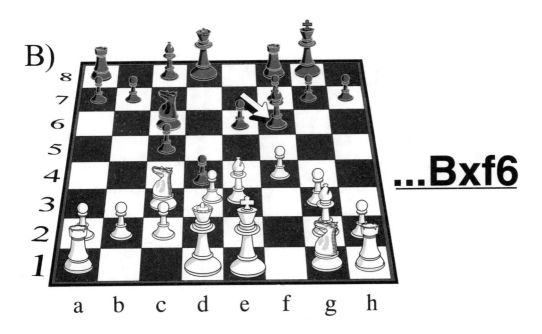

...Bxf6

6　Getting Started

Remember:

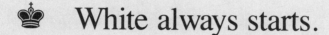

- ♚ White always starts.
- ♚ Protect your King.
- ♚ Look for good moves that get your pieces attacking.

Set your board
to play
your own game.

Which pieces can move on the first move?

Put a "✔" on all the pieces White can move to start the game.

Did you mark all the pieces?

Now "✔" all the pieces that Black can move.

All the pawns or the Knights can move on the first turn.

7 A Real Game

Many players look at other people's games to get good ideas. You can find games in newspapers, chess books, and chess magazines. The game in this section will give you practice in reading chess notation, and in playing through a complete game.

Use your board and chess set to play through this game, move by move. Playing it through will show you how to:

- develop pieces
- move pieces during a game
- capture pieces
- "trap" enemy pieces and the enemy King
- "mate"

The game was played September 9, 1992, at the Morris County Chess Club in New Jersey.

White was Bill Petersen. Black was Roz Katz.

Move 1.e4

1...c5

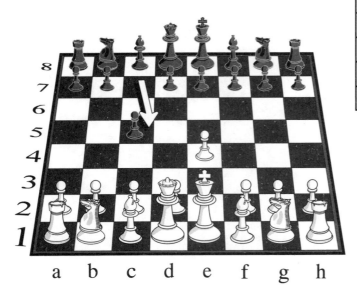

	White	Black
1	e4	c5
2	Nc3	Nc6
3	g3	Nf6
4	Bg2	e6
5	d3	Be7
6	Be3	0-0
7	f4	d5
8	e5	d4!!
9	exf6	Bxf6
10	Ne4	dxe3
11	Nxf6+	Qxf6
12	Bxc6!?	bxc6
13	Rb1	e5
14	fxe5??	Qf2++

2. Nc3

2 ... Nc6

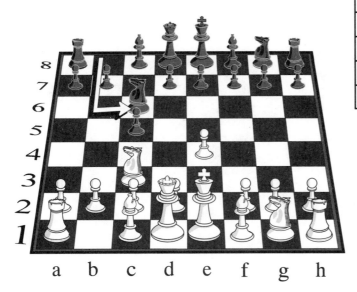

	White	Black
1	e4	c5
2	Nc3	Nc6
3	g3	Nf6
4	Bg2	e6
5	d3	Be7
6	Be3	0-0
7	f4	d5
8	e5	d4!!
9	exf6	Bxf6
10	Ne4	dxe3
11	Nxf6+	Qxf6
12	Bxc6!?	bxc6
13	Rb1	e5
14	fxe5??	Qf2++

3. g3

	White	Black
1	e4	c5
2	Nc3	Nc6
3	g3	Nf6
4	Bg2	e6
5	d3	Be7
6	Be3	0-0
7	f4	d5
8	e5	d4!!
9	exf6	Bxf6
10	Ne4	dxe3
11	Nxf6+	Qxf6
12	Bxc6!?	bxc6
13	Rb1	e5
14	fxe5??	Qf2++

3 ... Nf6

4. Bg2

4 ... e6

	White	Black
1	e4	c5
2	Nc3	Nc6
3	g3	Nf6
4	Bg2	e6
5	d3	Be7
6	Be3	0-0
7	f4	d5
8	e5	d4!!
9	exf6	Bxf6
10	Ne4	dxe3
11	Nxf6+	Qxf6
12	Bxc6!?	bxc6
13	Rb1	e5
14	fxe5??	Qf2++

5. d3

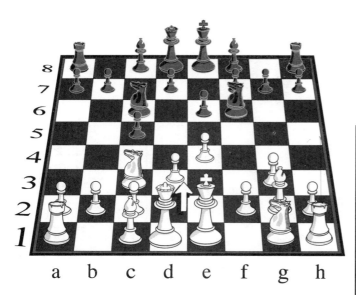

5 ... Be7

	White	Black
1	e4	c5
2	Nc3	Nc6
3	g3	Nf6
4	Bg2	e6
5	d3	Be7
6	Be3	0-0
7	f4	d5
8	e5	d4!!
9	exf6	Bxf6
10	Ne4	dxe3
11	Nxf6+	Qxf6
12	Bxc6!?	bxc6
13	Rb1	e5
14	fxe5??	Qf2++

6. Be3

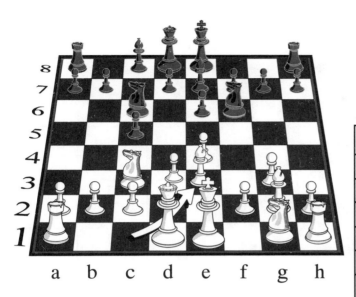

6 ... 0-0

	White	Black
1	e4	c5
2	Nc3	Nc6
3	g3	Nf6
4	Bg2	e6
5	d3	Be7
6	Be3	0-0
7	f4	d5
8	e5	d4!!
9	exf6	Bxf6
10	Ne4	dxe3
11	Nxf6+	Qxf6
12	Bxc6!?	bxc6
13	Rb1	e5
14	fxe5??	Qf2++

7. f4

7 ... d5

	White	Black
1	e4	c5
2	Nc3	Nc6
3	g3	Nf6
4	Bg2	e6
5	d3	Be7
6	Be3	0-0
7	f4	d5
8	e5	d4!!
9	exf6	Bxf6
10	Ne4	dxe3
11	Nxf6+	Qxf6
12	Bxc6!?	bxc6
13	Rb1	e5
14	fxe5??	Qf2++

8. e5

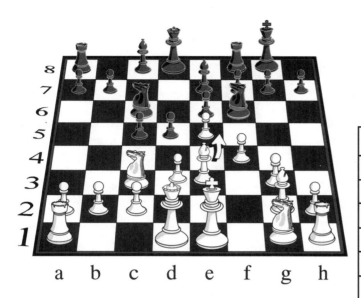

8 ... d4!!

	White	Black
1	e4	c5
2	Nc3	Nc6
3	g3	Nf6
4	Bg2	e6
5	d3	Be7
6	Be3	0-0
7	f4	d5
8	e5	d4!!
9	exf6	Bxf6
10	Ne4	dxe3
11	Nxf6+	Qxf6
12	Bxc6!?	bxc6
13	Rb1	e5
14	fxe5??	Qf2++

9. exf6

9 ... Bxf6

	White	Black
1	e4	c5
2	Nc3	Nc6
3	g3	Nf6
4	Bg2	e6
5	d3	Be7
6	Be3	0-0
7	f4	d5
8	e5	d4!!
9	exf6	Bxf6
10	Ne4	dxe3
11	Nxf6+	Qxf6
12	Bxc6!?	bxc6
13	Rb1	e5
14	fxe5??	Qf2++

10. Ne4

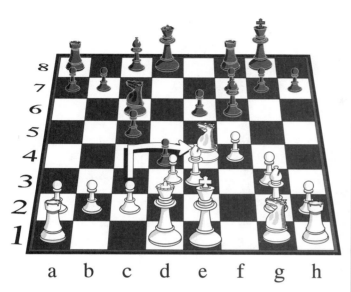

10 ... dxe3

	White	Black
1	e4	c5
2	Nc3	Nc6
3	g3	Nf6
4	Bg2	e6
5	d3	Be7
6	Be3	0-0
7	f4	d5
8	e5	d4!!
9	exf6	Bxf6
10	Ne4	dxe3
11	Nxf6+	Qxf6
12	Bxc6!?	bxc6
13	Rb1	e5
14	fxe5??	Qf2++

11. Nxf6+

11 ... Qxf6

	White	Black
1	e4	c5
2	Nc3	Nc6
3	g3	Nf6
4	Bg2	e6
5	d3	Be7
6	Be3	0-0
7	f4	d5
8	e5	d4!!
9	exf6	Bxf6
10	Ne4	dxe3
11	Nxf6+	Qxf6
12	Bxc6!?	bxc6
13	Rb1	e5
14	fxe5??	Qf2++

12. Bxc6!?

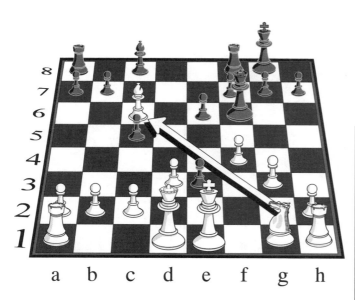

12 ... bxc6

	White	Black
1	e4	c5
2	Nc3	Nc6
3	g3	Nf6
4	Bg2	e6
5	d3	Be7
6	Be3	0-0
7	f4	d5
8	e5	d4!!
9	exf6	Bxf6
10	Ne4	dxe3
11	Nxf6+	Qxf6
12	Bxc6!?	bxc6
13	Rb1	e5
14	fxe5??	Qf2++

13. Rb1

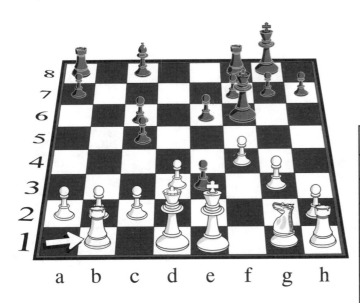

13 ... e5

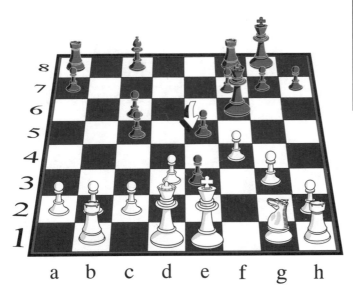

	White	Black
1	e4	c5
2	Nc3	Nc6
3	g3	Nf6
4	Bg2	e6
5	d3	Be7
6	Be3	0-0
7	f4	d5
8	e5	d4!!
9	exf6	Bxf6
10	Ne4	dxe3
11	Nxf6+	Qxf6
12	Bxc6!?	bxc6
13	Rb1	e5
14	fxe5??	Qf2++

14. fxe5??

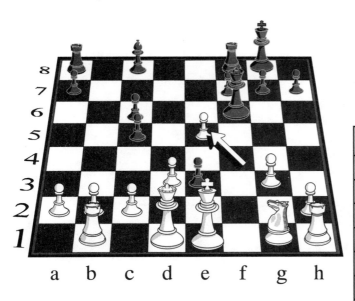

14 ... Qf2++

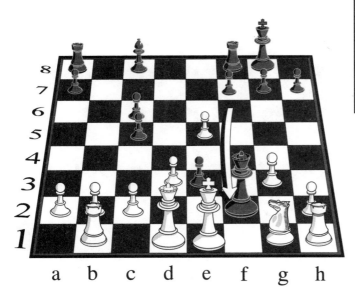

	White	Black
1	e4	c5
2	Nc3	Nc6
3	g3	Nf6
4	Bg2	e6
5	d3	Be7
6	Be3	0-0
7	f4	d5
8	e5	d4!!
9	exf6	Bxf6
10	Ne4	dxe3
11	Nxf6+	Qxf6
12	Bxc6!?	bxc6
13	Rb1	e5
14	fxe5??	Qf2++

8 Playing Tips

1. **Get your pieces out fast!**

2. **Castle to make your King safe.**

3. **Learn how to DRAW a game.**

4. **Move your King after most pieces are off the board. The King is strong in the endgame.**

5. **Think about your move. Don't move too fast.**

6.   Guess the other player's move.

7.   Write down your moves.

8.   Get other players to look at your games.

9.   Join a chess club, or start one.

10.   Be brave. Don't be afraid to make a risky move.

11.   Have fun!!

Next Steps in Chess

Chess players who want to get better, and who want to play seriously, play in tournaments.

You can get a magazine called *School Mates* by writing to the United States Chess Federation, 188 Route 9W, New Windsor, NY 12553.

Many schools have chess clubs. Some even have chess classes. If your school has no chess program, ask your teacher or parent to help start a club.

Index